Bad Hair Days, Rainy Days, and Mondays

Wisdom and Encouragement to Lift a Woman's Spirit

Cynthia Bond Hopson

DIMENSIONS
FOR LIVING
NASHVILLE

BAD HAIR DAYS, RAINY DAYS, AND MONDAYS
WISDOM AND ENCOURAGEMENT TO LIFT A WOMAN'S SPIRIT

Library of Congress Cataloging-in-Publication Data

Hopson, Cynthia A. Bond, 1955-

Bad hair days, rainy days, and Mondays : wisdom and encouragement to lift a woman's spirit / Cynthia Bond Hopson.

p. cm.

ISBN 0-687-49618-7 (pbk. : alk. paper)

1. Christian women—Religious life. 2. Devotional calendars. I. Title.
BV4844.H65 2006
242'.2—dc22

2005032958

Scripture quotations marked (NIV) are taken from the HOLY BIBLE, NEW INTERNATIONAL VERSION®. NIV®. Copyright © 1973, 1978, 1984 by International Bible Society. Used by permission of Zondervan Publishing House. All rights reserved.

CIRCLE OF LIFE
from Walt Disney Pictures' THE LION KING
Music by Elton J ohn
Lyrics by Tim Rice
© 1994 Wonderland Music Company, Inc.
All Rights Reserved. Used by Permission.

06 07 08 09 10 11 12 13 14 15—10 9 8 7 6 5 4 3 2

MANUFACTURED IN THE UNITED STATES OF AMERICA

T*he hopeful person sees success*

where others see failure,

sunshine where others see shadows and storm.

— O. S. Marden

Contents

Contents

A Word from the Author

Over the fifty years I have lived, I have learned a great deal about caring for myself as a woman. The first time I heard "pain is information," it hit me like a burst of arctic air because in my heart I knew it was true. Susan Taylor, then *Essence* magazine editor-in-chief, said it; and she admonished those who heard her to pay attention and do something about the circumstances and choices that brought us this pain. She probably saved my life because I realized that it wasn't just the physical "pain" that we needed to pay attention to, it was every aspect of our lives.

We give ourselves away at every turn. Maybe you are caring for a sick or invalid parent or child. Maybe you have a substance-addicted spouse, child, or sibling or a similar misery. Maybe the folk at work are working your last nerve. Whatever the case, the only person you can control is *you*, and the stuff and folk that worried you to death will still be here worrying somebody else long after we've admired how great you look resting there in your coffin.

I hope that when you pick up this book, you will find or make some quiet time to study and reflect. I have planned these lessons for contemplation and interaction—for you to make conscious and active choices about what comes next in your life. For each lesson, there is an accompanying scripture or quotation to complement it and a closing prayer.

Start today. Create some sacred time, space, and energy to be what God created you to be—beautiful, spirit-filled, fulfilled, at peace with yourself—even if it takes reciting the Serenity Prayer daily to stay that way. God is wise, sovereign, and gracious and, according to the Scriptures, gives us new mercies every morning. Today is a good time to wake up, smell the cinnamon rolls, and enjoy the soft gooey ones from the middle with the extra icing instead of settling for the hard, crusty ones around the sides with the burned bottoms.

These lessons are here to guard and protect you. I have learned them, sometimes the hard way; but I learned them just the same. Trust me, these will bless and keep you. Live triumphantly and remember: *You are touched by grace.* Amen.

Dedication and Thanks

I thank and praise God for this time that I'll spend with you, and I dedicate this work to God who continues to bless and anoint me. I am grateful to my family and friends, especially my husband, Roger. He is my best friend, biggest fan, and most enthusiastic cheerleader. We have two beautiful and delightful children, a darling daughter-in-law, and two even cuter and smarter grandchildren. Further, I have the best parents and siblings on earth and some of the finest friends you'll ever find. A special thanks to my sister Linda and my friends Barbara, Nicole, Sophia, and Rochelle, who gave me their honest opinions about this work, and to Cheryl, Fred, and Ron who helped me connect the dots.

My parents instilled in me long ago the belief that with Jesus Christ I could do all things. That reassurance has kept me and kept me going over the years. I have tried to seek the will of God in my life, and I believe that this book is a gift from God. I hope it will bless you in the days to come.

Live triumphantly.

Look not back in bitterness, or forward in fear,
but stand in the wonder of the moment.
—J. Forney

1. Remember: Nothing Is Worth More Than This Day.

Scripture: Matthew 6:25-34

We borrow trouble. We do. We worry about things that almost happened, should've happened, and might happen, when God has everything under control, including what will happen to you today, all day. One of my favorite refrigerator magnets says something like this: "Remind me, Lord, that nothing is going to happen to me today that you and I together can't handle." It's true; no matter how big or how small the problems are, they can't take us down unless we allow them to. (Oh, go ahead and pray for all the stuff just in case the mountain doesn't know it's a molehill.)

God has not given us a spirit of fear. God wants us to live every day until we die. This day is a gift and once it is gone, it is gone. We can't recall it, and we can't change anything about it. Living with regret is time and energy wasted. Pray, listen to your heart, do what you believe is right, and then let it go.

It's pretty amazing that no matter how long you live, every day is new—you've never seen it before, you've never wasted the hours or minutes on useless folly before. The day is brand spanking new like a Buick on the showroom floor, shiny and fresh, just waiting for you to rev up the engine and take it for a spin. Don't worry about denting it, dropping a crumb on the seats, or driving too fast. The new car, like the day, was built to endure whatever comes. Go ahead, make today count; its ordinariness may be the real treasure. There are rare and priceless jewels in our world, but nothing compares to the beauty of this day.

Oh Lord, thank you for today. I will rejoice and be glad in it. Amen.

---

1. Lesson title is a quotation from Johann Wolfgang von Goethe.

What we view with pleasure we never forget.
—Alfred Mercier

2. Practice Saying No.

Scripture: Micah 6:8

The prophet Micah is trying to find out what pleases God, and God's answer is to act justly, love mercy, and walk humbly with your God. I know the times have changed, but nowhere in this scripture (or any other one for that matter) is there a directive to serve on every darned committee in the church, community, neighborhood, and workplace. Nowhere does it say you need to be gone every night hauling your children to dance, choir, karate, and cooking classes. You're tired and worn out, and so are the children and the car. Sit down and take a breath.

Say the word *no*. It rhymes with *oh, dough, mow, go, doe*—you get the idea. You won't go up in smoke, nor will anybody else. Say, "No, I'm sorry, but I've got something on my calendar," and make sure that at the beginning of every month you write the word *something* on a couple of dates so that you won't be lying. Take yourself to lunch. Go to a local cosmetology school and get a manicure, a pedicure, a facial. Wander around aimlessly at the mall and take in a movie. Better yet, sit and look out the window. You might see a gorgeous sunset or a spider web glistening in the morning sun. The clouds might even dance for entertainment.

Don't wake up one morning and wonder where your life went because you've been consumed with "busyness." You've done a million and one things you disliked, grumbled about, or genuinely hated. Before you say yes again, ask: Is this something I really, really want to do? Will I enjoy it? If the answer is even close to no, delegate this task. Some roles we have to play, others we play by choice. When you do things you don't like or want to do, there is less time for doing what you do want to do. Don't waste time on things you neither enjoy nor are good at.

Lord, order my steps in every direction and show me what pleases you. Amen.

*We are what and where we are because we have
first imagined it.*
—Donald Curtis

3. Make Good Choices.

Scripture: Joshua 24:14-24

J oshua was about to lose patience with the Israelites because they couldn't stay focused and were not making good choices. They were doing an awful lot of moaning and whining because all the roads looked alike and they all seemed right, so which path should they take?

I volunteered at a neighborhood school last year with Miss Wendy's kindergarten class. She was so patient and kind to the children that I told her I wanted to be like her when I grew up. She never raised her voice or harped on their misdeeds. She simply spoke calmly and said, "Make good choices." And so we all must. We have to forget about other people's expectations and be clear about what our purpose and priorities are. We can't do everything, nor does the Lord expect us to.

We should set boundaries—they show us where to start and end. Forgive yourself, others, and circumstances. Choosing to give hate and misery a breeding place is a conscious choice. Don't do it. It is a losing situation. Don't repeat that gossip. Certainly you can choose to be a peacemaker instead of a troublemaker. You can choose to wallow in your disappointments, or you can choose to take the lemons and make the li'l suckers into lemon meringue pie, lemon pound cake, lemon chess pie, and lemon cookies. Take off your Wonder Woman belt before that thing cuts off your circulation. When in doubt about which choices to make, see lesson 2.

Lord, you have shown us your power to save, sustain, and defend us in times of uncertainty and distress. Help us rely on you and trust you with our dreams and hopes; for while life is full of choices, we know that choosing you is the only one that gives us peace, contentment, and eternal life. Amen.

There is a time for everything,
and a season for every activity under heaven:
. . . a time to be silent and a time to speak.
—Ecclesiastes 3:1, 7 (NIV)

4. Remember the Sabbath Day and Keep It Holy.

Scripture: Exodus 20:8; Ecclesiastes 3:1-9

In many Christian homes we think of Sunday as a Sabbath day, and we go and do formal worship or rest from the week's work. It is sometimes difficult for us to understand the "rest" part of Sabbath, but it too is key to our spiritual well-being.

I see many students working too many hours, enrolling in too many classes, and they seem to forget about their family's demands and their own need for rest. I tell them, "You can do all the things you're doing, but you're not going to do them well, nor are you going to get out of this alive." Pretty harsh words, but it is a wake-up call for those who don't understand that there is a direct correlation between rest and the things we want to accomplish.

I worked on my doctoral degree for four years, and it worked on me for the next three. By the time I finally finished, I had logged a million miles on my car and my body. I was exhausted, but I kept pushing. When I almost died about three weeks before graduation, my doctor insisted that I stay home and rest. During that time I discovered how heavenly doing nothing could be. I made a pact with myself and God after that: at least one day a month I would stay in my pajamas and in the house all day, with the phone turned off, and I would rest and not feel guilty. Surprisingly enough, the world has not come to an end. I find that after I emerge from my Sabbath I am more centered on God and in control of my life decisions. Perhaps one day a month is more than you can spend, but at least take an afternoon or an hour. Send your children to the neighbor, and offer her the same treat next week. Whatever it takes, create some space for you and God. This is not a luxury; it's survival.

Dear Lord, amidst the "busyness" of the world, help me create a time and place of rest. Help me treasure the beauty of doing nothing. Amen.

The more you know, the less you believe.
—Chinese fortune cookie

5. Do Not Give in to Flattery.

Scripture: Romans 16:17-20

F lattery has been described as "the art of patting people on the back in order to turn their heads." We've
all done it, and had it done to us—a well-placed, string-
attached compliment meant to elicit cooperation and
compliance. Sometimes the flatterer is so good we don't
realize we've been suckered until it is too late. (I once
traveled ninety miles to sing "Amazing Grace" because the
caller said no one else could do it like I do.)

Don't bake your prize-winning jam cake with that
"scrumptious caramel frosting" if doing so further com-
plicates your weekend. Hang up the phone or walk away
quickly before the guilt patrol arrives to remind you that
your cake is always the first to disappear, that the recipe is
the one the governor's wife insisted on having, and so on.

Better yet, smile sweetly, hand over the recipe, and say, "That cake is awesome, isn't it? If you have any problems, call me." There, you did it. You got lots of kind things said about you, and you didn't end up with any new tasks.

Most of us have a hard time distinguishing between flattery and compliments. Compliments have no strings attached and are to be graciously accepted. Here's a compliment: "Wow, that dress looks so good on you." Perfect and desired response: "Thanks, you are kind to say so." A simple thank you affirms you and the compliment giver. It's not anybody's business how old your dress is or how little or how much it cost. The same goes for your hair—if it looks great but it's dirty, let that be your little secret.

We all like to hear genuine praise and appreciation; however, the key is to watch out for the strings so you don't get wrapped up, tied up, and tangled up in something you didn't see coming.

Lord, thank you for the kind words I hear and can give to others along the way. I will look for opportunities to offer them sincerely. Amen.

Courage is not letting our fears control our actions.
—Anonymous

6. Take Care of Yourself.

Scripture: 2 Corinthians 7:1; Mark 5:25-34

I f some part of my body hurts, there's a reason, and I'm not satisfied until I find out what's wrong. I don't like surprises—if I've got the heebie-jeebies, I want to know. I have learned over the years that when my body talks, I should listen; so I schedule an annual physical exam and mammogram. When I go, I remind the nurse of the deal we made eighteen years ago on my first visit—if I weigh more this time than last time, she is to write that wicked number down without discussion or comment. If I weigh less, she should tell me everything. Of course, I take off my shoes and jacket just to be on the safe side.

Our health, however, is really no laughing matter. Getting a Pap smear, doing monthly breast exams, and watching your diet and blood sugar levels just puts you in the driver's seat. So many things can be cured if they are discovered early. It literally makes me sick when I hear of women who don't tend to themselves until they are almost beyond treatment. Do you not know? Have you not heard? You are the heart of your home—without you, it would be a different, lonelier, more chaotic place. You are the cog in the wheel, the flakes that the sugar frosting goes on, the bread for the peanut butter and jelly—you get the picture.

My heart ached when the wife of one of our friends died last year. Our friend said, "I'm writing on the back of bill envelopes because I don't even know where Susan kept the clean paper." We knew it wasn't just about the clean paper—he was completely lost without Susan.

Your family and friends need everything about you—your wit, good sense, warm hugs, insight, honesty, essence, presence, and a chicken leg every now and then. Your health is a gift from God. Cherish and protect it for the treasure it is.

Lord, thank you for all that makes me uniquely me. I am wonderfully and miraculously made, and I know it. Help me treasure and care for myself so that I may continue to hear and do your will. Amen.

It is not easy to find happiness in ourselves,
and it is not possible to find it elsewhere.
—Agnes Repplier

7. Relax Your Standards.

Scripture Reading: Luke 10:38-42

I remember a time when I could not rest until everything in my house was in order. Every sock had to be matched, every plate and fork had to be in the cabinet, and never would there be a panicked look or frantic scurrying if the doorbell rang unexpectedly. OK, so it was a long time ago; but I can sort of vaguely remember it.

Somewhere along the way, wall and floor scrubbing and spring cleaning fell by the wayside. What took their place was what my great-grandmother used to call "a lick and a promise"—do what's absolutely necessary now and promise to do better later—much later. You heard it here first: If you don't dust, mop, and vacuum every day, the furniture and carpet last longer. (No, it's not scientific—sue me.) And I learned that if there are dirty glasses in the sink at bedtime, they will be there in the morning—the dirty glass munchkin does not employ elves to wash them during the night.

I'm not sure when my priorities changed, but at some point I realized there were sweet babies I could cuddle and read bedtime stories to, dates I could go on with my husband, lunch and shopping trips I could take with my friends, novels I could read, and a million other fun things to do. I decided these things were more important than cleaning off the top of the refrigerator just in case somebody dropped in. My motto became: If you're coming to see me, come on in, move stuff, and have a seat. If you're coming to see my house, call way ahead.

We don't know how long we will live, so it is critical that we do things that really matter. Refuse to live with regret. I promise you that the table that needs dusting today will need another dusting a week from now. Skip the dusting and see a movie. You won't be sorry.

Lord, you know I am not lazy when I don't gather every speck of dust. You have helped me discern what really matters, and I thank you. Amen.

If you're going to run with the big dogs,
you've got to invest in some good flea powder.
—Cynthia Bond Hopson

8. Get Organized.

Scripture: Matthew 6:19-21

Treasure is a funny thing—the Scriptures say that where our treasure is, that's where our hearts are. Look for both my heart and treasures in an attic box labeled "stuff," because I have had a hard time defining and letting go of treasured things that now clutter my life and me.

The unknown author who said "Order is heaven's first order and earth's last achievement" must have mumbled this while packing to move. Recently my mother and I cleaned out my great-aunt's one-room apartment when we moved her to a nursing home. She had pay stubs from the 1950s, empty medicine bottles, and all manner of things she had kept. My mother would ask, "Why do you think she kept this?" We both went home and pledged to clean out closets, dresser drawers, and cabinets and only save stuff that would "really" matter.

You should too. First, rearrange those places that attract clutter—for me it was the kitchen table and the spot by my chair. I had articles for class, comic strips, and coupons; but I never found anything without searching everything, every time. Second, fix it by using file folders, bins, and labels. Third, get a huge garbage bag. After seven years, old tax records are just that—old. Shred the sensitive information and dump the rest. Fourth, multitask: organize dresser and file drawers, clip coupons, or sort photos while you're watching TV or videos. Fifth, have a yard sale—remember the "one woman's trash is another's treasure" rule. Sixth, put things that have sentimental value in a safe, special, easy-to-remember place—chuck the rest.

Here's a measuring stick to use: Do I absolutely, positively love this? Is it an heirloom? Will anybody give a sweet doggone about it in twenty-five years? If no, get busy on your last earthly achievement, maintaining order so you can thrive and grow.

Lord, help me simplify and unclutter my life. Help me know true treasure when I see it. Amen.

We are sometimes taken into troubled waters
not to drown, but to be cleansed.
—Barbara Ann Kipfer

9. Find a New Rhythm for Your Life.

Scripture: Matthew 25:14-29

Over the past fifty years, the Lord and I have had long talks about where the Lord was taking me. Some of those talks came at my lowest points; others came when the roof opened up after the doors and windows had slammed shut. I finally surrendered, saying, "Lord, I don't know what you're doing in my life, but you do. Help me be patient." Surrender meant trusting God completely to give me the "talents" to multiply; to supply all my needs, no matter how big or small they were; and to give me peace through it all.

In 1987, I had a job I was beginning to loathe. I was miserable and so was everyone around me. My husband begged me to find something else to do and stop whining. I quit work and began graduate school. One Sunday I did the children's sermon at church; and our friend Rosemary said, "You have a real knack for teaching." I looked at her like she had three purple heads. Teaching was not on my agenda. All I knew about teachers was that they gave tons of homework and reported to parents when you misbehaved. Even that little bit of knowledge convinced me that teaching was not for the fainthearted.

Anyway, as graduation neared, I prayed and finally applied for media and teaching jobs. The reply letters were kind, but they all said no—except Lane College. I called Lane every day until I got hired to teach, and I haven't "worked" a day since. Some days I have so much fun that I feel guilty taking my pay.

You too must find a rhythm that makes you sing. Start your own business, whether it's consulting, baking yummy chocolate chip cookies, or making fancy window treatments. Just do it—if you make one step, the Lord will make two. Plan your work and work your plan. Step out on faith. If you think you can, you can—all the clichés work here. You only live once, so don't be miserable with your life or your work. Enjoy the scenic route as you trust God with everything that concerns you.

Lord, you know I am scared to death of change, but I will follow wherever you lead. Amen.

Enjoy what you have; let the fool hunt for more.
—Anonymous

10. Learn from the Mistakes of Others.

Scripture: Proverbs 15:2-3, 7; 16:13, 16

I have discovered that wisdom is like pregnancy—either you are wise or you're not. My favorite T-shirt was designed with me in mind. It says, "In order to be old and wise, you must first be young and stupid." Amen.

When you're young and know everything, it is hard to see when people are trying to save you from yourself and the world. Ezell—Lord, I loved that man. I was seventeen. He was cute and twenty-seven, had an ex-wife and a child, and had literally been around the world and back when I met him. My parents said he was way too old, and he was only after one thing. They wanted me to go to college and see the world, not get tied down so young. They said, "You haven't been anywhere and done anything yet." All I could hear were the sweet nothings he whispered in my ear. We were madly in love, and that was that. Well, after a while I finally figured out we didn't have the same goals and dreams. As for the other part, well, trust me when I say my parents may have been wise indeed.

Every experience offers an opportunity to grow and learn, whether exponentially or in small increments. Some lessons we have to suffer personally. Others we profit from vicariously. In either case we're supposed to live, learn, and not keep making the same stupid mistakes. If we must make mistakes, and we all must and will, at least let's find new ones.

Do your research, and trust your heart and your gut. If *it* (whatever *it* is) doesn't feel right or sounds too good to be true, pay attention. If you're thinking about taking your retirement money and lending it to your friend's son who doesn't have a job or any visible means of support— go slowly. If your fiancée doesn't respect you or your dreams and is always berating you, listen when we tell you to pay attention. Run as fast as you can down the road less traveled—it'll make all the difference.

Lord, help me hear wise words that will spare me unnecessary heartache and pain. Help me seek your guidance; and when the hard lessons come, let me learn from them and grow stronger in your care. Amen.

*If you buy happiness on installment,
the payments last much longer than the happiness.*
—Barbara Ann Kipfer

11. Know Your Bugs and Stones.

Scripture: 1 Peter 1:3-9

One songwriter wrote: "Some days are diamonds, some days are stones." Another put it this way: "Some days you're the windshield, some days you're the bug." If it's going to be a bug or a stone day, at least take precautions so you don't get mashed flat or tossed in the stream.

I used to believe that if you minded your own business, people would leave you alone. I know now that ain't necessarily so. Sometimes minding your own business just gives other people fodder for their foolishness and allows time for evil to fester. Some days all you can do is muddle through. Some days will be so hard and your burdens so heavy that you can barely make it, but God knows you and knows where you live. As I often say, "Despite how things look right now, nothing has happened to you today that the Lord doesn't know about."

You can't predict what others will do, and you can't keep mean-spirited people from doing what they do, so stop trying. All you can do is live so that nobody believes them when they weave their web. Once somebody told me an awful tale about one of my friends. I emphatically said, "I don't believe it. That doesn't sound like the Luci I know; and unless she tells me with her own mouth, I won't believe it." It stopped that person and that awful lie in their tracks.

All we can do is (1) try our best and live the best we know how, (2) treat everyone with love and respect, (3) know that we can't control every circumstance because there will always be somebody who doesn't do what they're supposed to do, (4) roll with the punches, and (5) know that for every rain cloud there is a rainbow . . . even if you're a bug.

Lord, help me know what day it is, and help me appreciate the stones as much as the diamonds. And Lord, if it's my bug day, let me be a ladybug (cute, friendly, and persistent) or a firefly (shining brightly). Amen.

All the flowers of all the tomorrow
are in the seeds of today.
—Chinese Proverb

12. Be an Acorn.

Scripture: Jeremiah 29:11-14

Neither Rome nor the world was built in a day. That's comforting to know, because sometimes while we're on our way to being "pure gold," we lose heart. We want to be this or we want to be that; and if it's not happening yesterday, we want to take matters into our own hands. Here's what we need to know: God is going to be God, and when God says there are plans for you—trust me, there are plans; but they will unfold in God's own time. And while we may have deserved that promotion last year, or want to get that new home next month, maybe it isn't time. One of my favorite southern gospel songs says, "I read the back of the book and we win." That's all you need to know. The Lord's got this, whatever *this* is.

In a recent magazine article, Asbury Seminary President Jeff Greenway chronicled how he came to his position. He said he prayed the following two prayers almost daily: "Lord, help me to be more like Jesus tonight when I go to bed than I was when I got up this morning," and "Lord, please take my life and let it have maximum impact for you wherever you place me."[1] To his surprise, he found that he wasn't going where he thought he was going. He had had no plans to be a seminary president; but he came to understand that he had to be open to new and different directions, and so we must too.

Today, the UPS truck came by and left a box I thought was another children's lunchbox for my husband's million-box collection. (No, we didn't eat that many lunches.) Instead, inside were copies of my newest book, *Times of Challenge and Controversy.* I cried. Many times I had asked the Lord to deliver me from the fields, but the cotton just got thicker and the rows got longer. I had never dreamed of writing books. I wanted to be like Della Street on TV's *Perry Mason* or Gail on *Mannix.* Wow, an acorn indeed. God has plans for you too. Enough said.

Take my life, Lord, and let it be a testament to all of your mighty works and grace. Amen.

---

1. *Asbury Herald,* 115, no. 1 (2005): p. 3.

Your body is a temple, not an amusement park.
—Anonymous

13. Honor Your Mind and Body.

Scripture: 1 Corinthians 6:19-20

I love Cynthia Ann. There, I said it. I was not struck by lightning, the world did not come to an end, nor were any world wars started as a result of my declaration. Somewhere along the line we were told to love our neighbors, friends, and family; but the part about loving ourselves got buried.

I was at the mall a couple of weeks ago, and someone at the cosmetics counter brightly asked if I'd like a makeover. I told her no; it's taken a long time to become me. I can define and stand up for myself. I know (most days) what I want to do, and then I do it. Maybe it happened when I turned forty, but I stopped worrying if people approved of my choices. You're welcome to say that you don't like my hair short, but it's my head. You think I shouldn't wear pearls with that outfit? Tough. I like them and they make me feel like Jacqueline Kennedy, so there.

I try to eat healthful foods. (Okay, I'm a sucker for peach cobbler and warm pound cake, but they don't count.) I *intend* to exercise regularly. I surround myself with positive thoughts and people. Whenever I can, I shun things and folks who stress me. The scripture above affirms the value in these choices.

We must guard our minds and bodies against negativity, decay, and disease. My husband's former secretary, Mary Muzzall, would say, "I hope my body doesn't outlive my mind." We laughed but realized that many of us take a sound mind and body for granted. Whether you live to be 8 or 108, you can keep yourself alert and vibrant. Take a walk. Sit, admire the morning, and gather your thoughts; then you can conquer the world. Explore new places and possibilities so you'll see the wonder God has created. Watch *Jeopardy*. Play a little Scrabble. Go to a lecture at a local college. Take a nap and rest so your body and mind can be refreshed.

Honor is a nifty word—we can have it and do it for ourselves. That beats a makeover any day.

Lord, we honor you when we honor ourselves. Help us glorify you with our praise. Amen.

There is one who knows the road
Who'll help us carry, . . . our heavy load.
—Dr. W. Herbert Brewster

14. Learn to Let Go.

Scripture: John 11:1-44

I have a whole new understanding of what suffering means. This understanding came as I watched illnesses take their toll on my loved ones. My beloved Uncle Carey was stricken with cancer. One day he went to bed seemingly normal, and the next it looked like he took off sixty pounds with his clothes. My dear father had a heart attack on September 4, 2004, and died. As author Lewis Grizzard would say: "It took my heart out and stomped that sucker flat." During the meal after Dad's service, I had to retreat to the quiet of my parents' home, because I knew that if one more person said, "Don't cry" or "Be strong," I'd never stop screaming. Now I smile whenever I think of my father or hear his favorite song.

I have never lost a child, but people who have say that you define everything in terms of before and after the loss. One friend said she stayed in bed and cried for six months after her daughter died. Another said she visits her son's grave every Wednesday, and it's been fifteen years. Some days, she can't get going at all. The process of letting go gets redesigned and redefined every time, and there are no right or wrong answers about how to do it. When I realized that my dad would never have to suffer again, it was a powerful release for my heart and soul and I rejoiced. The Scriptures tell us that there is a season for everything, and so there is a time for living and a time for dying and a time for letting go. No matter what the trial, God will always give us the strength and courage we need.

The lessons we learn from grieving will help us minister more effectively to our friends and loved ones in their times of need. For example: What do you take with you when you visit a bereaved family? Answer: Yourself, along with everyday items (foil, garbage bags, paper towels, and tissues) and ready-to-eat or easy-to-prepare foods in sensible proportions (think one bucket of chicken rather than three). However, the important thing is just being available with hands and hugs.

Don't make your visit a one-time occurrence. Pray, call, and come by the next week and the next week. Bring postage stamps, a small box of thank-you cards, and more hugs. Remember bereaved families on holidays, anniversaries, and birthdays; I dreaded my first Father's Day without Dad, and there was nothing I could do to escape all the advertising.

Of course, grief isn't the only thing we need to let go of; but it may be one of the toughest. Work at your own pace, and God will be there every step of the way. I promise.

Lord, tenderly heal and hold our hearts. With your help, we can be strong again. Amen.

When you take time to listen to the dreams of a child, you are giving the most important gift of all.
—Flavia Dayminder

15. Listen to the Children.

Scripture: Luke 9:46-48; Matthew 18:1-5

When Elise told me, "You act just like a child," I didn't quite know how to take it. When she grinned and said, "But that's a good thing," we became immediate friends, even though she was eight and I was forty-one. My adult friends think I'm a little weird, but I love hanging out with little people and can carry on a conversation with almost anybody's child, no matter where I find them.

Little people are nifty, and if there's anything more wonderful than the laughter of a happy child, I don't know what it might be. One of my favorite movies is *The Color Purple*. I've watched it enough to know the lines by heart, and I always ache for Mister after Miss Celie finally gets the courage to leave him. He wanders around his place and laments, "Ain't no chirren, ain't no laughter." He's right—children transform us and our spaces. We smile more and are more willing to behave; and their energy, honesty, and curiosity keep us hopping.

I don't ever remember my parents telling me that they treasured me, but I knew it by the way they treated me and by the example they set. We all have that same responsibility, whether we have children or not. My favorite quote comes from that beloved author, Anonymous, and it says: "One hundred years from now it will not matter what my bank account was, the sort of house I lived in, or the kind of car I drove; but the world may be better because I was important in the life of a child."

In my own life I decided that being "important" would look like this: I would speak to children in the same tones as I would my peers; model good behavior so the "monkey see, monkey do" part takes care of itself; look at music videos and listen to some of "that" music, whether I enjoyed it or not, so I could at least know what issues it raised; encourage and affirm children and parents for treating each other with dignity and respect; be an advocate for justice and equal rights for children; and invest energy to stem risky behaviors.

Can and will we save every child? Probably not, but do this for me: Find a new little friend at church or borrow one from a neighbor or your local school. (The school will do a background check, but that too is a good thing.) Go to lunch and a movie with your new friend, or better yet, sit and listen. You'll learn a lot. According to the Scriptures, this will please Jesus and make you "the greatest."

Lord, we know you love children, all the children of the world. Help us make each child our own, no matter where we find them or whose they are. Help us guard and guide, love and protect them. Amen.

*Real friends are those who inspire you to dream,
and help you to become more
than you could have imagined.*

—Anonymous

16. Make New Friends, But Treasure the Old.

Scripture: John 15:10-17

Lois and I have been best friends since Mrs. Haley's second-grade class. That means we lived through having no front teeth, stuffing our bras with tissue (okay, so it was just my bra), having babies, everything. Aundria and Marcos, our oldest, were born exactly two months apart. To say we are close is like saying every face has a nose; and even when I don't see her often, we resume where we left off. Our circle has expanded over the past forty-three years, but we are still bound by love, respect, and her momma's li'l biscuits.

Love, respect, and shared experiences are the glue that binds friends. When your mouth says, "I'm fine," they can tell from your eyes whether you're lying. They have been with us all night for all kinds of reasons and have taken us places nobody else knew about. They know where all the bodies are buried because they furnished the shovel, but they won't tell even if they can remember. If you want an honest assessment, run things by them. If that tight, red dress makes you look like a sack of potatoes, the salesperson may lie but friends never will. The Scriptures described them right—friends are those who are willing to sacrifice for you.

The research is conclusive: Women who have supportive friends are much happier and live longer, richer, fuller lives than those who don't. At first one of my friends was flattered that her boyfriend wanted her all to himself, and he convinced her she didn't need "all of them" hanging around. She reluctantly let us go and kept him. It wasn't long before he was abusing and controlling her. We helped her take off the rose-colored glasses and see more clearly.

All of us learned lessons from that experience. Don't let anything separate you from your friends—not work, relationships, distance, nothing. You need the fellowship, love, care, and honesty as much as you need air and water. True friends are hard to come by—when you find real ones, keep them forever.

Lord, thank you for wonderful friends who enrich our lives. Let us be the kind of friends who can be trusted and depended on. Amen.

*Forgiveness from the heart is better
than a box of gold.*
                                        —Anonymous

17. Forgive and Set Yourself Free.

Scripture: Matthew 6:14-15; Mark 11:24-25

Hate is such a harsh word—I can still hear my high school teacher, Miss Wills, saying that to me one day. I was talking about hating something or the other, and she immediately interrupted with a wave of her hand to tell me that. More than thirty-four years later, I don't ever use that word without thinking of her and the word's power. *Hate* is the kind of word that when you say it, negative images emerge and linger. Oftentimes, images of people who hate or that you hate come forth too.

For more than five years I hated Orville Lewis Henry.[1] He had lied and humiliated me, and I hated him. Pure, simple, and full-time. I knew hating him was wrong, and I prayed that I wouldn't die before I got around to forgiving him. One day I realized that maybe it wasn't all his fault. I asked God to forgive him and me and let me move forward. I felt more free than I had in years, and I immediately knew a heavy burden had been lifted from my heart and mind. Somebody had once told me that hatred does more damage to the vessel in which it is stored than to the object on which it is poured. I didn't want to hear it and I sure didn't believe it, but it's true.

Over the years I've learned that there is no hope or salvation in hate and holding grudges. Hate will eat you alive and will eat away at you like acid. If you expect to be whole, you must let the hatred go. Energies spent on getting even or hating could and should be better directed at something useful. I've also learned that you cannot hate and pray for the same person—asking the Lord to bless and zap somebody cannot co-exist in the same sentence. They may not change, but you sure will. President John Kennedy put it this way: "Forgive your enemies, but don't forget their names." That's fine, but the first order is to forgive and move on. Do it today and keep doing it until there is no more hate. The world and you will be better.

Lord, help me forgive my enemies and myself. When hatred threatens to cloud the way, replace it with love and kind thoughts. Amen.

---

1. As they used to say on the TV show *Dragnet*, names have been changed to protect the innocent.

*Success is to measured not so much by the position
that one has reached in life
as by the obstacles . . . overcome.*
—Booker T. Washington

18. Understand That It Is All Right to Fail

Scripture: Romans 15:1-6; 1 Peter 1:2-9

I don't like to fail. And while I know that it's impossible to be good at everything, if I don't think I'll be good at something, I just don't try it. Understand that this George Bernard Shaw quote—"A life spent making mistakes is not only more honorable but more useful than a life spent doing nothing"—has not been a part of my life.

My Graduate Record Examinations scores were low because I don't do well with standardized tests. That didn't keep me from graduating with my master's degree; however, at the next level, the low scores were keeping me from being accepted into a doctoral program. I applied to a new program at the University of Alabama. It would be about four hours away, but I thought I could manage it and keep working. When the admissions people saw my scores, they basically said thanks, but no thanks. It didn't matter that my grades and letters of recommendation said I was smart—the low scores meant no admission.

I was devastated. The rejection made me feel like my whole life had been a failure. I called Roger and tearfully recounted what the admissions people had said. He calmly reminded me that if that door had closed, God must be ready to open a window some place else. Sure enough, Southern Illinois University had an admissions policy that took into consideration all these other factors, and I was accepted.

That Booker T. Washington quote about how success is to be measured reminds me of our sixteenth president, Abraham Lincoln. Dear Abe had failed at virtually everything he tried before he was twice elected president. Thomas Edison said he wasn't a failure—he just knew lots of ways not to make a light bulb. We must be inspired by our failures, pushed forward by our weaknesses. With God as the wind beneath our wings, there is no telling where we will be or who we will become. Let's soar!

Lord, thank you for the struggles that come to make us strong. With your love and care, we will heal, endure, and become strong from our storms. Amen.

In the middle of difficulty lies opportunity.
—Albert Einstein

19. Look for Healing from Childhood Wounds.

Scripture: Matthew 9:18-35

S ometimes I am a little slow, and it takes a minute for me to "get it"—for my elevator to go all the way to the top. I knew that my parents instilled values and high morals with their teachings, but they were so wonderful that I thought all parents were like mine. Then one summer I was doing some reading for a class and came across an article about imprisoned women.

I knew there were women in prison, but I had never had to give much thought as to why or how they got there. The author told how many girls are molested or raped by their fathers, brothers, stepfathers, mother's boyfriends, or other men in their lives. Many of these girls run away, end up on the street, or do whatever they have to do to survive, including drugs and prostitution. I was numb for a week. As I kept reading, other authors described the hell children live in with alcoholic or drug-addicted parents. Then I served on a children's home board and watched the movie *The Cider House Rules*. I tossed the rose-colored glasses and "got it."

Popular advice columns confirm that many of us have been so scarred and crippled that we can't walk, run, or soar. Too often we escape childhood homes filled with turmoil and violence, and then we choose lovers who shove us back to the place we were running from. Rejection, pain, isolation, abuse—whether physical, emotional, or chemical—all take a toll on who we are and who we can become. It may take years before we are whole again, but we can be. It takes a conscious decision, patience, professional help, and time; but we can heal.

If you seek healing, it may be helpful to find somebody you can trust and who can listen without making judgments. Don't keep suffering in silence and shame. Gospel singer Tramaine Hawkins said many years ago in a song called "The Potter's House" that "you don't have to stay in the shape that you're in—the Potter wants to put you back together again." Don't keep being broken and battered. Seek refuge.

Lord, you are a healer and a friend—we need both today. Give us your care and your courage. Amen.

If I can help somebody as I pass along,
If I can cheer somebody with a word or a song,
If I can show somebody that they're traveling wrong,
Then my living shall not be in vain.
—Alma B. Androzzo

20. Lend a Hand.

Scripture: Galatians 6:9-10; Hebrews 12:12-16

I intend to do great things before I die. I'm not sure what that includes, but I want the world to be a better place because I lived. Mother Teresa said that it is not how much you do but how much love you put into doing and sharing with others that is important. So, how will I leave a lasting impact, a legacy? The answers seem simple—give, serve, and care.

Linda Bloodworth-Thomason and her husband Harry created television sitcoms in the late 1980s and early 90s and made lots of money. She started a foundation for women who had dreams but no means to make them come true. She has said she wants to die broke. Talk show host Oprah Winfrey started a similar foundation, as did early industry barons such as the Carnegies, Rockefellers, Rosenwalds, and Woodruffs. They endowed schools and built libraries and arts centers. Mother Teresa served children and lepers in Calcutta, and Mother Clara Hale provided shelter and love for drug-addicted and abandoned babies.

I thought about these people with money or a lifelong commitment. Their feats seemed overwhelming. Then I heard of an eighty-five-year-old woman in my community who begins her day picking up trash in front of her home and in her community. I heard another story about someone who helped children plant gardens in housing projects, and one about a woman who collected prom dresses for young women who couldn't afford them. Small deeds done with great love—yes, indeed.

What will be our legacy? It might be mentoring young women. When my sister earned her Ph.D. at age thirty-one, she helped steer me to mine; and now I help others. Your greatest legacy may be the straight talk you do with the youth in your church or community to keep them away from drugs, teen pregnancy, and other risky behavior. Whatever you do, if it's from your heart and meant to help, it will. Do what you can with what you have. Think of what Jesus did with two fish, five loaves, and a crowd of five thousand. Expect a miracle.

Lord, I want to give and do my best. With your blessing, great things can and will be done, and the glory and praise will be yours. Amen.

*Oh, the places you will **go!***
—Dr. Seuss

21. Go West, Young Woman; and While You're at It, Go East, North, and South Too.

Scripture: Romans 15:23-33

hristopher Columbus and I would have been big friends since we are both explorers at heart. I have a car with gasoline and air conditioning and he didn't, but the concept is the same—exploration. I honestly believe that the Lord created stuff just for me to find. When I see a road, I'm much more likely to go see what's down there than not, and I have found lots of interesting places just wandering down roads. I have been to Christmasville, Nankipoo, Curve, Stella (okay, so there wasn't much to see, but I was there), and points far beyond. I make sure I have daylight and a full gas tank, then I'm off for an adventure.

My husband and I are on a quest to visit all fifty states and the other six continents before we die or get too old to get in the car or on a plane. So far, I'm missing New Mexico, Connecticut, Delaware, Rhode Island, Utah, Idaho, Nebraska, Oklahoma, and a couple more; but we have seen covered bridges in Vermont, admired the big Montana sky, marveled at a South Dakota sunset, gasped at the snow-covered mountains of Colorado, touched the Aboriginal people of Australia, experienced the excitement of South America, and encountered the peace and turmoil of Africa. In every place God has taken us, we have seen God's hand at work; and I come home more focused and refreshed.

I think I was bitten by the "go" bug when I was a child growing up on a farm surrounded by trees, chickens, hogs, cows, cotton, and not much else. I read and dreamed about far-off places. My teacher, Miss Sophronia Wills, traveled during her summers, and she'd enthrall us with stories from her jaunts. Inspired by her, I decided to go and do things. I encourage you to go and do too. A song from the movie *Lion King* says:

From the day we arrive on the planet
And blinking, step into the sun
There's more to see than can ever be seen
More to do than can ever be done.

It's true, so we've got to get busy. It really doesn't cost that much if you're thrifty and plan ahead. Save your odd dollars or your candy and soda money. If your check is $67.98, save $7.98 for the "go" fund. If you're using a credit card, get one with points that convert to air miles or rental cars. Sign up for hotel plans where if you stay for a night, you get a night free. Don't let the world pass you by—go this weekend, this summer, this winter, but go. As the poet Robert Frost says:

I have promises to keep,
And miles to go before I sleep.

Lord, thank you for an adventuresome spirit. I praise you for the places you send me and the opportunities you provide. I will go, if you lead me. Amen.

Love is never lost. If not reciprocated, it will flow
back and soften and purify the heart.
—Washington Irving

22. Fall in Love.

Scripture: 1 Corinthians 13:4-8

As I sat in my favorite spot watching the robins play and admiring the morning, I wondered where my husband had gone so early. He soon returned, laden with grocery bags. He explained that he wanted me to have my favorite orange juice (with pulp) and fresh Cheerios. Now, understand we had other cereals and orange juice without pulp, but he wanted to make me happy. *Lord,* I thought, *thank you for this sweet man.*

And God is responsible. My sister Norma deserves credit for introducing us, but it was God who brought us together. I'm sure of it. Remember Ezell from lesson 10? Well, we were supposed to live happily ever after, but it didn't work out; so I was not looking for a boyfriend when Roger showed up. He tricked me into going with him to his P.E. class that sunny day back in June; and while he should have been taking notes, he was passing notes to me. He swears I took his breath away, but I wasn't ready to be serious. He was hard to resist, though, because he was cute and witty. That July he announced we were getting married.

I couldn't argue, because he made me laugh, hadn't bored me to tears, and seemed to be going places. He loved doing things for me so I decided, *Girlie girl, he's a keeper.* More than thirty years later, he still is. We cherish, honor, and adore each other. He insists I argue for the sake of argument and that I'm always putting his stuff somewhere and can't remember where; but he and the lost-sock munchkin are friends, so there. Nevertheless, at the end of the day, I know he's the one I'm planning to hang out with for the next one hundred years.

Like a lot of stories in real life, this story has more than one moral: (1) Love is a gift from God; don't settle for less. (2) Look for someone with similar dreams so you get to the same place. (3) Find someone who will affirm you. (4) Know who you are so you know who you're looking for. (5) Be friends first, and ask yourself, *Do I like this person?* Love is one thing—like is another. (6) Skip the math. Whoever said love is 50/50 had never been married or in a relationship. Sometimes it's 60/40 or 70/30; but if you are grounded in faith, you can weather any storm.

(8) Work at your marriage just like you do your job—go on dates and deliberately plan intimate time. Love makes all the difference—let's wallow, exhale, and bask in it.

Lord, we know that you surround us with a great love—love that is endless, patient, kind, and perfect. We will share it. Amen.

Mama may have, Papa may have.
But God bless the child that's got his own.
—Billie Holiday / Arthur Herzog, Jr.

23. Have Your Own Money.

Scripture: Proverbs 31:10-28

I work hard so I can get some of the things I want." I've heard these familiar words as long as I can remember. They come from my great aunt/mother Emma who has worked hard her whole life and always has some money. She bakes, quilts, fixes a little hair—you name it, she can do it, and she can reaallly stretch a dollar. She'd admonish us, "Don't have to ask a man for money, and don't ever let a man know how much money you've got." She said that whoever controlled the purse strings, whether it was government or individuals, could tell you what to do and not to do.

Take care of your money. Save some of it, no matter how little you think you have, and always keep a twenty- or fifty-dollar bill in your wallet for hard times. If you're not savvy about how to make your money work for you, call a trusted expert. At the same time, do not save everything for a rainy day—enjoy yourself. I've told my children that if there's anything left when I die, they can have it; but I'm not working to leave stuff behind for them to enjoy. I don't save my best stuff for company; I share it with them. Don't be too stingy to eat or too cheap to buy what you want.

Tithe. Tithing is your gift to God; and I've learned that when you do this first, you'll always have enough. I have tithed since my first job, and it still tickles and amazes me to see the Lord work. Tithe yourself—commit a portion of your time each week to making and managing you better, whether it's by reading, museum hopping, or listening to profound thoughts. Soak it all in and grow.

Finally, only lend money you don't want returned and to people you don't care about because if they don't repay you like they said, they will make themselves real scarce. Don't co-sign either because if they don't pay, well, you know the rest of that story.

Lord, thank you for blessing us with what we need. Help us to use resources wisely and to be good stewards of all that you provide. We want to be wise, generous, virtuous, and blessed today. Amen.

A hairdo on a woman's head is even more changeable than what's on her mind.
—Anonymous

24. Don't Let Bad Hair Days, Rainy Days, and Mondays Get You Down.

Scripture: Luke 12:22-31

I don't know who coined the phrase "bad hair day," but they probably caught me on the wrong day and thought "Lord, she sure needs something done to her head." And when my hair isn't right, ain't nothing right. My whole mood is wrong. My grandmother always said, "A woman's hair is her glory," a paraphrase of the Scriptures; and she was right. If your head and your hair are in order, you can put and keep all your other challenges in perspective. If they're not, you need all the help you can get.

For instance, I have yet to see a day that mashed potatoes and gravy couldn't improve. When I'm down and out, I'm looking for comfort food and reassurance. I am like the cartoon character Popeye, who got his strength only after he opened a trusty can of spinach and ate it straight out of the can. I'm the same way when I'm wearing my favorite black dress or after I've had mashed potatoes and gravy. They shout, "Don't mess with me."

It's the same with doilies. When I was a child, we had these beautiful handmade doilies (or dresser scarves, as they are sometimes called) all around. They had to be washed and meticulously starched so they could set under the lamps and things. I never gave them much thought until I saw them at antique shops; but somehow they reminded me of home, a safe place. I started buying them and putting them on my chair backs and under lamps and on the table and bookshelves. Now they adorn my office, and my students and I enjoy their homey feel.

What does it for you? Maybe it's gooey chocolate, a well-worn afghan, ratty pajamas, a favorite song, a funny television show, or scruffy shoes that lean so you have to lay down to put them on. Whatever it is, claim it. Coupled with prayer, these things help us make sense of the day and of the events that threaten our sanity.

Lord, thank you for comfort food and doilies. In the grand scheme of things they probably don't matter much, but they remind us of your care and love and make us strong again. Amen.

A woman who will tell her age
will tell just about anything.
—Anonymous

25. Bask in Your Age.

Scripture: Proverbs 9:10-11; Luke 5:39; 12:35-36

I thank the Lord that I'm getting better every year. When I look at my li'l homely pictures from high school and the early years—whew! My best days must be ahead of me. Yes, it took me a while to find the road to marvelous and magnificent, but I found it. I don't remember what I wanted to be when I grew up—I just wanted to be "grown" because grownups seemed to have all the fun. I couldn't wait to be 13, then 18, then 21 and 25, and before I knew it, I was 40. I am sure I wished and squandered away many of my youthful years trying to live before my time.

And yes, I tell my age because I am so excited to be alive, and I think we need to celebrate. Aunt Velma was such a fabulous role model. The Christmas before she died at 87, she arrived for dinner in red leather pants and a matching fur jacket, holding hands with "Odell," who was 74. She was interesting and interested, and I'd tell her I was going to be like her when I grew up. There was nothing old about her. Her attitude and insight made her a delight.

Some people grow up; others simply grow old. I want all of us to be in the first group. I want us to blossom and grow, learn and flourish, spread our wings and soar! We can do this by celebrating who we are and where we've come from. When I talk about being from the cotton fields, I'm not just making conversation. The values I learned—work hard, be honest and honorable, follow the Golden Rule—these tenets have been the foundation of my success. I have also learned to value people more than things, to see and care for people where I find them, and to serve as a means of grace.

It doesn't matter if you're 9 or 97, bask in who God has allowed you to become. Every day you live, you have a chance to do some good and to be a blessing. Oh, and for good measure, get yourself some red leather pants with a matching jacket so you can strut your stuff.

Lord, thank you for guarding and keeping us day by day. We are basking in your glory and your faithfulness. Amen.

What I have may not be much,
in the eyes of someone else.
It may be limited by human frailty . . .
but all that I have, I give it, Lord, to thee.
—Gospel Song

26. Know That You Are Beautiful

Scripture: Psalm 139:13-18

Oh Lord, it's hard to be humble
when you're perfect in every way.

The words from that Mac Davis 1970s hit are right. We are perfect in every way. We are chilled Sprite Remix and hot chocolate chip cookies—it really doesn't get any better.

Whether you've got a cute nose like I do, or perfectly arched brows like I don't without help from the world's greatest barber, Damion, when you appreciate your beauty, you're bragging on God, not yourself.

Sometimes at retreats I ask women to name five things of beauty about themselves. They look at me like I've asked them to dissect an elephant on the dining room table. They tell everything except about themselves, and it's probably because we are so hung up on the things we don't like—our hips and feet are too large, breasts are too small—the list could go on for hours.

I don't know where my cute nose came from; but when my sister Norma and I visited Aunt Sallie in the nursing home recently, she didn't immediately recognize us, but she said we belonged to her because we had her nose. We giggled because we did; but I also have nice hands, a pleasant voice, beautifully shaped lips, my grandmother's legs, and "big, pretty arms," in Aunt Sallie's words. Not fat arms, but big, pretty ones. She has a wonderful way with words.

We are a collection of arms, legs, hips, and things, but beauty doesn't just come from our physical appearance. It's what's inside that makes us special, virtuous, and extraordinary, as extolled in the Scriptures. It's how we treat ourselves and those we love. We must be good and kind to ourselves and celebrate our own beauty in our own skin, whether we've got freckles, unwanted facial hair, a squeaky voice, or ears that stick off our head. We are a reflection of God; so go ahead, get close to the mirror, grin real big, and wink at that beautiful image staring back at you.

Lord, thank you for making us in your own image. Yes, you are awesome and worthy to be praised. Amen.

You can't do anything about the length of your life,
but you can do something about its depth and width.
                                                    —Anonymous

27. Live Until You Die.

Scripture: Luke 23:34a

E very man dies, but not every man truly lives." This line from the movie *Braveheart* haunted me from the moment it was spoken. It made me wonder what kind of living I was doing. Was I planning and wasting my life away? Was I wallowing in shoulda, woulda, coulda? Was I so busy complaining about what I didn't have that I forgot to treasure what I had? Was I squeezing every drop out of today just in case tomorrow never came?

The Scriptures tell us that we don't know how long we will live or when it will be our time to go, so we must live until we die. But how do we do that? Nobody sets out to waste time, but you wake up one day and you're seventy-nine and you wonder, *Where did the time go?* Since I'm only fifty, here are some of the things I think it takes to live well: (1) Make your own decisions and listen to your heart, not someone else's. Find work that's satisfying and that you would do for free. (2) Handle your own business. Don't leave serious decisions to other folks. Make a will for living and dying so that if you can't speak for yourself, your family will know your wishes. Pick out your own assisted living facility just in case you need it. (3) Refuse to live with regret.

At fifty, I'm taking up piano after I return from Hawaii and Alaska. And I'm going to listen to the thought that represents the philosophy of Methodist pioneer John Wesley: Do all the good you can, by all the means you can, in all the ways you can, in all the places you can, at all the times you can, to all the people you can, as long as ever you can. When I've done all these things, I'll be ready to go.

On the eve of her debut on *Oprah*, actress, model, and artist Corey Burton said to a reporter, "I always wanted to travel my own road. I just didn't know how." She's not alone; most of us don't know how either. Let's define, stalk, and conquer our own destiny, on our own terms; and let's do that by living every day like it's our last. Let's ride the waves, whether they take us into deep water or over the top. Then, if tomorrow never comes, we'll be satisfied.

Lord, help us travel our own road, wherever it goes. Amen.

It is possible to fly without motors, but not without knowledge and skill.
—Wilbur Wright

28. Know Who and Whose You Are.

Scripture: Psalm 139

I 've stopped saying I can't do math, because I can. True, I'm no whiz; but I never thought the Lord created me to be a mathematician. For years, though, I did try to figure out what my "gifts and graces" were. I kept looking for something lofty and great, but what I discovered was that the Lord had given me a gift to work with people. Give me a hundred people, and I can get along with ninety-nine and a half of them.

Over the years the Lord has shown me that my people gift is important and special. One day at a conference someone told me, "You brought the sunshine with you." I had never noticed. When my husband was a pastor, I often accompanied him when he visited parishioners because I loved meeting new friends. When I worked in banking, I got roses from one of my drive-through customers because I had made him feel welcomed and appreciated. I finally realized that this was a precious gift and I should use it for God's glory.

Whether you've found your place in the sun or not, know that what you were created to do, nobody else can do. Your words of encouragement may be the only ones that that harried mother of four gets today. Your organizing skills may be just the lift your office or the church library needs. If you can figure things out quickly and act decisively, trust me, these are gifts from God. In the military, bridge builders build bridges. They don't fly jets or fix heavy machinery, they build bridges. Maybe that's your gift. Some families have Grand Canyon-sized holes, and your role as peacemaker and bridge builder can be a blessing.

If you haven't yet discovered why you were created, get in the Lord's way like Zacchaeus did. It may take fire and hail before your true purpose is revealed, but understand God loves and cares for you and is anxious to hear that you're willing and ready to take on your work.

Lord, show us your will and your way for our lives. We are waiting, yielded and still. Amen.

*Great works are performed not by strength
but perseverance.*
—Samuel Johnson

29. Salute Your Heroes.

Scripture: Matthew 20:20-28

E ver since I was a child, I have wanted to be an action hero. I wanted to rush into burning buildings, kick a little bad-guy butt, rescue the kidnapped damsel, and ride off on my trusty white steed or in the Batmobile. I wanted to be like Wonder Woman and have a cool costume and use my golden lasso to whip the pesky criminals back into line. It took me a really long time to realize that all of those television feats do not a hero make. Heck, if it were easy, we would have so many Batmobile dealerships we'd have to build new factories to assemble them. And if you're working so people will think you're great, they probably won't.

Heroes come in all shapes and sizes. If we define them right, they're all around us. They're my great-grandmother, who was widowed with two children in 1929 but made it anyway. They're my maternal grandmother, who at age fifty-six passed the GED for her high school diploma. They're my paternal grandmother, who admonished us to persevere and finish what we started. They're my great aunt/mother, who was forward-thinking enough to chronicle our community's history through the collection of artifacts such as pictures and funeral programs. They are mothers like mine, who invested their lives into their families and communities.

Heroes are parents, aunts, uncles, neighbors, teachers, ministers, ministers' spouses—the villagers who have invested time and resources in us to make us and the world better. They're you and me, because for somebody we may be the only hope, the rescuer on the trusty steed. We can see far because we are standing on the shoulders of giants. God created and sustained them, and they prayed and sacrificed for and dreamed of a better day for us. We can do the same for the generations to come, not because we want to be great but because we serve a great and awesome God.

Lord, we want to serve and please you, not so we will be great but because you are. We are standing on your promises; help us go the extra mile and see with our hearts instead of our head and eyes. Amen.

Personally I'm always ready to learn,
although I do not always like being taught.
—Sir Winston Churchill

30. Learn Something New Every Day.

Scripture: 2 Timothy 3:10-17

My beloved great-grandmother Irene P. Jones often told me, "There's enough you don't know to make a whole brand-new world." As a child I suspected that, but she was right. Sure, some things you learn as you get older, but the key is trying to figure out what you think you already know.

I was talking to my friend Rochelle's eight-year-old, Michael, and he was discussing the climate in Hawaii. I asked him how he knew that, and he just looked at me as if to say, "Doesn't everybody?" What are they teaching kids these days, I wondered—climate, oceans, habitat, whew!

Anyway, learning is a wonderful, magnificent, amazing thing—and the more you know, the more you understand there's still more you don't know.

Thankfully I discovered early that I could learn a lot by listening and paying attention. I took mental notes about who had what, where they got it, what they did with it, and how the game was played. I learned a few of the unwritten rules too. I learned to surround myself with books and all kinds of people, because each offered a rich new experience.

Here's what all that taught me: (1) There is no way to learn everything, no matter how long you live, so learn all you can. (2) No matter how much you know, there is always somebody who knows and can do more. Get over it. (3) Nothing significant will ever be created without passion and enthusiasm, no matter what the instructions said. (4) Read everything you get your hands on—can labels, dictionaries, encyclopedias, *everything*. (5) If you don't know, say so. Honesty counts. (6) Learning something new every day makes your brain happy and improves your looks. The first part I can prove—the last part, well, it could be true. Why not take a chance?

Lord, let me learn more and more about you and your transforming love. Show me how to serve and please you as I grow in grace and knowledge. Amen.

Laugh I say, for laughing is happiness,
leave behind your sorrows,
Laugh to heal your wounds,
laugh to send away your troubles,
Laugh to allow the body to grow in health and vigor,
Laugh in order to rise should you fall.
—Shabaan Roberts

31. A Giggle a Day Keeps the Doctor Away.

Scripture: Psalms 23; 126:1-3; 128:1-2

About six years ago I could hardly get going, so I called my doctor. She took one look at me and asked, "What's going on with you?" I assured her she didn't have a year for me to tell her. She pulled up a stool and said, "Try me." I told it all, including about the time I stole lemon cookies in fourth grade. She let me finish, then got up and wrote a prescription for a book called *The Value in the Valley: A Black Woman's Guide Through Life's Dilemmas,* by Iyanla Vanzant. She hugged me and said come back in two weeks.

I stumbled to the bookstore and opened the book to the first page. Vanzant simply said that sometimes we're so busy trying to get out of the valley, we miss the lessons the Lord is trying to teach us. She said to seek God's guidance where we are instead of hurrying through the valley. I prayerfully asked, "Lord, what do I need to learn today?"

The Lord showed me that the promises made long ago—never to leave me or forsake me; always to be my comfort and guide—were still true. So it is with all of us. We all have trials, whether we're battling cancer, depression, or upheaval at home, at work, or at church; but the promises are still true. So many times we expect a new boyfriend, a bigger home, or a cure-all concoction to restore us, but the joy that produces laughter comes from inside.

Laughter is a gift from God and it comes from indescribable joy. It's cheap and affordable. Recent research even shows that it's good for your heart too. Laughter can come when we know and understand that God wants us to be happy and content. One of our friends has such an infectious laugh that hearing her makes us laugh. I love telling stories that my aunts Florence and Ira Lee told, or listening to my mother and Uncle Willie recreate voices from their childhood.

Today, laugh so hard that your sides hurt and your eyes water. Get the kind of tickled that makes you feel like you're bursting inside. Laugh—it may save your life, the way my doctor's hug and prescription did. Remember: A giggle a day keeps the doctor away.

Lord, thank you for planting joy in our hearts daily. Remind us to spread it and delight in you and in the sound of our own laughter. Amen.

Quotation by Shabaan Roberts from *My Soul Looks Back, 'Less I Forget: A Collection of Quotations by People of Color,* edited by Dorothy Winbush Riley (New York: HarperCollins, 1993).

Self-respect comes to us when we are alone, in quiet moments, in quiet places, when we suddenly realize that knowing the good, we have done it; knowing the beautiful, we have served it; knowing the truth, we have spoken it.
—Alfred Griswold

Famous Last Words

A person who walks in another's tracks leaves no footprints.
—Anonymous

Teach us love, compassion and honor so that we may heal the earth and heal each other.
—Ojibwa prayer from *Every Part of the Earth Is Sacred: Native American Voices in Praise of Nature*

A dog's gonna need his tail more than once.
—Emma J. Bowles

Any plan that cannot be changed is a bad one.
—Barbara Ann Kipfer

Live and cherish every moment of today
as if there were no more tomorrows,
for there may not be.
—Cynthia Bond Hopson

Do what you can, with what you have,
where you are.
—Theodore Roosevelt

Enjoy all that you have and all that you are.
—Anonymous

T-h-i-n-k.
—John A. Bond, Jr.

Children really do live what they learn.
—Dorothy Law Nolte

There is no right way to do wrong.
—Elizabeth Knox

We will do nothing at all if we wait to be sure
that no one will be able to find fault
with what we do.
—John Henry Cardinal Newman